TRAVEL WITH THE
GREAT EXPLORERS

Explore with
Gertrude
Bell

Tim Cooke

Crabtree Publishing Company
www.crabtreebooks.com

Crabtree Publishing Company
www.crabtreebooks.com

Author: Tim Cooke

Designer: Lynne Lennon

Picture Manager: Sophie Mortimer

Design Manager: Keith Davis

Editorial Director: Lindsey Lowe

Children's Publisher: Anne O'Daly

Crabtree Editorial Director: Kathy Middleton

Crabtree Editor: Petrice Custance

Proofreader: Angela Kaelberer

Production coordinator and prepress technician: Tammy McGarr

Print coordinator: Margaret Amy Salter

Written and produced for Crabtree Publishing Company by Brown Bear Books

Photographs:
Front Cover: **Getty Images:** Hulton-Deutsch Collection/Corbis main; **Shutterstock:** cr, Sake van Petit tr; **Thinkstock:** istockphoto br.

Interior: Alamy: Cris Andrews/Oxford Picture Library 5l, Art Collection
3 4b, Chronicle 14r, 24, 28t, Lebrecht Music and Arts Photo Library 21b, 23, PhotoStock-Israel 26-27t, Royal Geographical Society 14bl, 19t, Vintage Archives 17t; **Bridgeman Art Library:** British Library 20; **Gertrude Bell Archives:** Newcastle University 11t; **Getty Images:** Bettmann 10, Cris Bouroncle/AFP 28bl; **Library of Congress:** 6, 24-25t; **National Railway Museum:** 4t; **Public Domain:** RGS/GB Archives 13b, 16; **Royal Collection:** 29b; **Shutterstock:** 7r, 13r, EcoPrint 22b, Sarah Lois 7t; **Thinkstock:** istockphoto 6, 20; **Topfoto:** 11b, 19bl, 25r, Alinari 33t, Granger Collection 12, 18bl, 18tr, 21t, Roger-Viollet 5r, 29t, Ullsteinbild 15b, 16-17b, 27b.
All other artwork and maps, **Brown Bear Books Ltd.**

Brown Bear Books has made every attempt to contact the copyright holder. If you have any information please contact licensing@brownbearbooks.co.uk

Library and Archives Canada Cataloguing in Publication

CIP Available at the Library and Archives Canada

Library of Congress Cataloging-in-Publication Data

Names: Cooke, Tim, 1961- author.
Title: Explore with Gertrude Bell / Tim Cooke.
Description: New York : Crabtree Publishing Company, [2018] | Series: Travel with the great explorers | Includes index.
Identifiers: LCCN 2017028415 (print) | LCCN 2017028878 (ebook) | ISBN 9781427178091 (Electronic HTML) | ISBN 9780778739104 (reinforced library binding : alk. paper) | ISBN 9780778739258 (pbk. : alk. paper)
Subjects: LCSH: Bell, Gertrude Lowthian, 1868-1926--Juvenile literature. | Travelers--Middle East--Biography--Juvenile literature. | Women travelers--Middle East--Biography--Juvenile literature. | Archaeologists--Great Britain--Biography--Juvenile literature. | Women archaeologists--Great Britain--Biography--Juvenile literature.
Classification: LCC DA566.9.B39 (ebook) | LCC DA566.9.B39 C66 2018 (print) | DDC 956/.02092 [B] --dc23
LC record available at https://lccn.loc.gov/2017028415

Crabtree Publishing Company
www.crabtreebooks.com 1-800-387-7650

Printed in Canada/092017/PB20170719

Published in Canada
Crabtree Publishing
616 Welland Ave.
St. Catharines, ON
L2M 5V6

Published in the United States
Crabtree Publishing
PMB 59051
350 Fifth Avenue, 59th Floor
New York, New York 10118

Published in the United Kingdom
Crabtree Publishing
Maritme House
Basin Road North, Hove
BN41 1WR

Published in Australia
Crabtree Publishing
3 Charles Street
Coburg North
VIC, 3058

CONTENTS

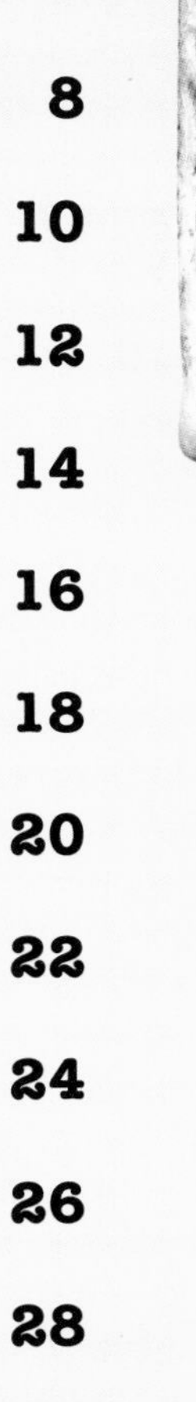

Meet the Boss

Gertrude Bell (1868–1926) was born into one of the wealthiest families in Great Britain during the reign of Queen Victoria. A woman of her class was expected to become a wife and mother, but Gertrude had other ideas.

Did you know ?

Gertrude's father, Sir Hugh Bell, was a supporter of trade unions, public libraries, and schools. His desire to treat people fairly shaped how Gertrude interacted with peoples in the Middle East.

WEALTHY FAMILY

+ Born into money

The Bells were said to be the sixth-richest family in Great Britain. Gertrude's grandfather, Sir Isaac Lowthian Bell (right), was a scientist. He used his knowledge to build the largest iron-working and coal-mining company in England. The business employed 47,000 people. The Bells were known for treating their employees fairly. Gertrude was brought up to believe it was important to look after less fortunate people.

DEVASTATING LOSS

- ★ **Loses mother age three**
- ★ **Close bond with father**

In 1871, Gertrude's mother, Mary, died after giving birth to Gertrude's baby brother, Maurice. For the rest of her life, Gertrude was extremely close to her father, Hugh (left), who brought up the children. Hugh and Gertrude were devoted to each other for the rest of their lives.

A HAPPY FAMILY

★ **Stepmother writes plays**

★ **Encourages Gertrude**

In August 1876, Hugh Bell married his second wife. Gertrude's new stepmother was 24-year-old Florence Olliffe, who was a successful playwright. Florence was also interested in social issues. She wrote a ground-breaking study on the lives of poor workers. Florence believed that it was not enough simply to talk about social problems. She taught Gertrude that people of their privileged background could become involved in improving the lives of others.

Education

Gertrude was very smart. At 15 she was sent to London, as her parents felt she needed a more challenging school. The teachers recommended Gertrude go to Oxford University, which was rare for women at the time.

FEMALE PIONEER

+ **Gertrude works hard**

Gertrude went to Oxford University in 1886 and studied at Lady Margaret Hall (above). It was one of only two Oxford colleges that admitted women. Not only did Gertrude graduate a year ahead of schedule, she also gained the highest mark of the year in Modern History. She was the first woman to ever achieve this. Her success was even announced in *The Times*.

A DIFFERENT COURSE

☛ **Breaking society's rules**

Gertrude was adventurous and independent. She also had ideas of her own about her future. She did not want simply to become a wife and mother, like other women of her class. Instead she wanted to travel and explore the world. She wanted to make a difference in the world and to help people.

Where Are We Heading?

After university, Gertrude traveled widely, including making two round-the-world trips. She found herself particularly drawn to the Middle East.

Did you know ?

Although Gertrude traveled widely, her main interest was the Middle East. She spent many years exploring and living in the deserts and cities of what are now Arabia, Syria, Iraq, and Iran.

A FIRST TRIP

- To Constantinople
- Via Bucharest

In December 1888, Gertrude made her first long-distance trip. She and her step aunt, Lady Lascelles, traveled to Bucharest in Romania to visit Gertrude's uncle, who was a British official there. From Romania, Gertrude traveled to the capital of the huge Ottoman **Empire**, Constantinople (modern-day Istanbul, above). Gertrude arrived in April 1889. She fell in love with the city. Constantinople marked the place where Europe and Asia met. It was her first contact with the Middle East.

GLOBAL TRAVELER

+ Circles the world twice

Gertrude had the traveling bug. She and her brother Maurice traveled around the world in 1897, and then again in 1902 and 1903. They stayed in the best hotels and traveled first class. On the first trip, they sailed across the Atlantic and then went on to Japan. On the second trip, they visited India before traveling east to Singapore, China, Korea, and Japan. They also crossed the United States, where Gertrude climbed in the Rocky Mountains.

INTO PERSIA

+ First visit to Middle East

+ Travels on luxury train

Before the first of her world trips in 1897, Gertrude got the chance to go back to Constantinople. In 1892 she traveled through Europe on the famous Orient Express, a luxury railroad train. From Constantinople, she went by boat to Tehran (above), the capital of Persia (now Iran). Gertrude loved Persia so much that she decided to learn Persian. When she returned home, she wrote a book about her travels. *Persian Pictures* was published in 1894.

My Explorer Journal

★ **Imagine that you are Gertrude Bell and that you are traveling on a luxury train. What sort of facilities do you think such a train should have, and why?**

ON TOP OF THE WORLD

☛ Enthusiastic mountaineer

Gertrude was a skilled mountain climber. She climbed many difficult peaks in Europe and North America, including the Matterhorn and Mont Blanc (above) in the Alps. The first peak she climbed, the Meije, was also in the Alps. It was 13,068 feet (3,983 m) high. Because women's clothing at the time was not suited for physical activity, Gertrude climbed in her underclothes! She later said that she was terrified. Despite several accidents, she kept climbing throughout her life.

TRAVEL UPDATE

Learn the Language!

★ If you want to get to know a place, learn to speak to local people. As Gertrude Bell became more interested in the Middle East, she spent many hours studying Persian. Later she went on to learn Arabic. Gertrude was a gifted **linguist**. She learned to speak both languages fluently enough to talk to everyone she met. At the time, it was unusual for a European to learn such languages—and especially a woman.

GERTRUDE BELL'S TRAVELS IN THE MIDDLE EAST

Gertrude Bell traveled widely in the Middle East. She visited the deserts and cities mainly for her own enjoyment, as a tourist. This map shows only some of the journeys she made.

Constantinople

Locator map

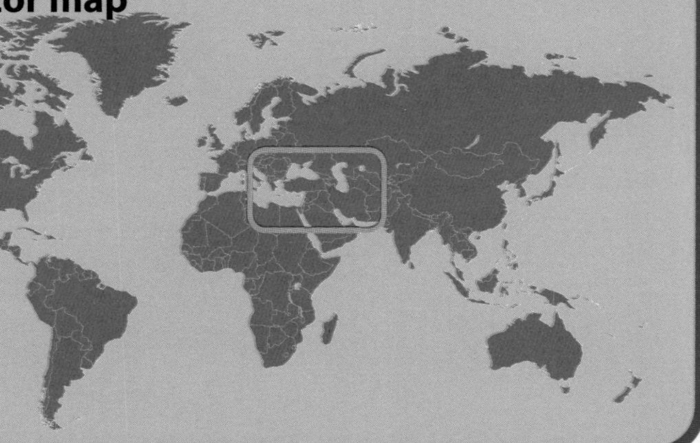

Cairo

EGYPT

Cairo

In 1921, the British held a conference in the Egyptian capital to decide the future of the Middle East. Gertrude Bell was the only woman among the 40 **delegates**. She recommended the appointment of the Arabian rebel leader Faisal bin Hussein as the first king of Iraq.

Constantinople

The capital of the Ottoman Empire stood on the narrow sea channel that separated Europe from Asia. From there the Ottomans ruled an empire that stretched across the Middle East. Ottoman control was weakening by the 1900s. Peoples within the empire were beginning to express hopes for independence.

Key

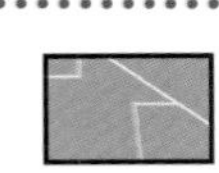

Main expedition

Modern national borders

Tehran

Tehran was the capital of the Persian Empire, or Iran. Gertrude visited in 1893, after her uncle was posted there as a **diplomat**. After World War I (1914–1918), the British tried to establish a **protectorate** there. Instead, the Iranians set up a new **dynasty** that ruled for most of the 20th century.

TURKEY

SYRIA

Palmyra

Tehran

Damascus

Baghdad

IRAQ

Hayil

ARABIA

Scale 0 400 miles 0 800 km

Baghdad

Baghdad was an ancient **Islamic** capital. When the British established a protectorate in Iraq after World War I, they made it the capital of Iraq. Gertrude Bell lived there for the last years of her life.

Arabia

The Arabian **peninsula** was home to the Islamic faith. Beginning in 1916, Arabs revolted against their Ottoman rulers and helped the British during World War I. After the war, the British ignored their promise to help the Arabs achieve independence. European powers divided up Arab lands and reorganized the Middle East.

Damascus

Damascus was the capital of Syria, which Gertrude described in her book *The Desert and the Sown* (1907). The book introduced many readers to the beauties of the Syrian desert.

Meet the Crew

Gertrude did not always get on well with people, as she could be demanding, but she had many good friends and was very close to her family.

Welcome

As a woman, Gertrude faced fewer restrictions in Arabia than she did in England. In Arabia, men greeted her as an equal because she spoke their language and understood their way of life.

A CLOSE FAMILY

+ Gertrude's biggest supporters

+ And traveling companions

Gertrude remained close to her father and brothers throughout her life. When she was traveling, they visited with her. She also wrote them many letters. She was also close to her stepmother, Florence, and often asked her advice. Gertrude's father, Hugh, and Florence (right) both outlived Gertrude. After Gertrude died, Florence **edited** her letters. It was a big job because Gertrude wrote letters nearly every day of her life.

UNLUCKY IN LOVE

★ Gertrude chooses work

Gertrude, like all women at that time, was expected to marry and have children. She first fell in love with a British official in Persia, but her parents disapproved of him. She then had another relationship, but that man died during World War I, leaving Gertrude heartbroken. She remained single the rest of her life, devoting herself to important work, which included playing a major role in the creation of Iraq.

A FAITHFUL SERVANT

+Fattouh looks after Gertrude

Gertrude traveled with servants who set up her camp in the desert. Her most reliable servant was Fattouh (right, with Gertrude), a Persian man who accompanied her on many expeditions. When Gertrude traveled to Arabia in 1913, Fattouh was too sick to go with her. She missed his help—he knew just how she liked her camp run. Later, when Fattouh left Gertrude's service, he was punished by the Turks for having worked for a European employer.

"It's so nice to be a spoke in the wheel, one that helps to turn, not one that hinders."
Gertrude Bell describes her role helping Sir Percy Cox in the creation of Iraq.

IMPORTANT OFFICIAL

- **Middle East expert**
- **Relies on Gertrude**

Gertrude first met Sir Percy Cox in 1902 (left, center) when he was the British **consul** in Muscat in Oman. They remained friends for the rest of her life. The British put Sir Percy in charge of setting up the new country of Iraq and appointing a ruler. Sir Percy relied on Gertrude's knowledge of the region to help him make important decisions. Unlike other British officials, he did not mind that Gertrude was a woman!

Check Out the Ride

Gertrude was born during a time of great change in travel. A skilled horsewoman, she also rode camels. Later in her life, the automobile and airplane became the chief modes of transportation.

Did you know ?

During Gertrude's lifetime, people went from riding horses to traveling by automobile or airplane. Gertrude used both these modern technologies on her travels.

THE ORIENT EXPRESS

+ Paris to Istanbul

Gertrude traveled on the famous Orient Express a number of times. This luxury train (above) traveled from Paris to Constantinople (now Istanbul), via Munich, Vienna, Budapest, and Bucharest. The journey took three days. Passengers had their own compartments and ate their meals in a dining car. There was a good chance of Gertrude meeting someone she knew onboard. Only very wealthy people could afford the journey.

TRAVEL UPDATE

Hitch a Ride!

★ If you're traveling during wartime, you can always try to get a **berth** on a troopship. That was what Gertrude did during World War I. She sailed from Egypt to India, where she wanted to meet the British Viceroy. But be warned, you might not get much warning of when the ship will leave. Gertrude got just three hours' notice to sail. In addition, troopships are crowded and not very comfortable!

Weather Forecast

INTO THE DESERT!

In the deserts of Iraq and the Middle East, the daytime temperature can reach 120° Fahrenheit (48° Celsius). When Gertrude Bell spent long periods in the desert, she took camels. On some trips, she used as many as 17 camels to carry the people and all the equipment. Desert peoples traditionally used camels to travel because the animals need little water to drink, and their thick coats protect them from the fierce sun.

My Explorer Journal

★ Imagine that you are Gertrude Bell. Which form of transportation do you think would be most useful in the Middle East? Give reasons for your answer.

RIDE LIKE A MAN!

- Gertrude loves horses
- But not sidesaddle!

Gertrude rode horses all her life. She was a skilled horsewoman. Women were supposed to ride sitting **sidesaddle**, rather than sitting astride, but riding for long periods sidesaddle was uncomfortable. Gertrude had a special skirt made that had slits up to the knees at the front and back so that she could sit in the saddle like a man (left). This was thought to be shocking!

Solve It With Science

Gertrude was fascinated by the ancient culture of the Middle East. Using the most up-to-date cameras, she captured this little known world and its people.

Maps

Gertrude's maps were later criticized for drawing straight lines that separated tribes unnecessarily. The nomadic way the tribes lived did not really fit with the idea of a country with fixed borders.

MAPPING THE DESERT

★ **Gertrude records her travels**

★ **Helps create a country!**

As Gertrude explored the deserts of the Middle East, she drew maps of the areas she visited. Some of these places had never been mapped before. In 1920, her maps were used to create the borders of modern Iraq. Gertrude knew, however, that the borders were not perfect. It was impossible to make everyone happy, so any new borders were bound to be compromises.

SNAP HAPPY

☛ **Enthusiastic photographer**

☛ **With the latest cameras**

Gertrude was a skilled photographer and always traveled with two cameras. She was a member of Britain's Royal Photographic Society. Gertrude photographed the sites she visited and the people she met (left), many of whom had never been photographed before. Today Gertrude's photographs are a valuable record of what the Middle East was like a hundred years ago.

DIGGING AROUND

★ **Passion for the ancient past**

★ **Mesopotamian artifacts**

Gertrude was an enthusiastic **archaeologist**. She dug up **artifacts** from ancient Iraq, or Mesopotamia (left). Mesopotamia was home to some of the world's first civilizations. Gertrude used methodical **excavation** and carefully recorded where she found objects. She later helped to create a national museum in Baghdad where the artifacts could be studied.

My Explorer Journal

★ **Gertrude cataloged the ancient artifacts she found for the museum. Find an item in your home and write a description of it as if it were being displayed in a museum.**

"I had a well-spent morning at the office making out the southern desert frontier of Iraq." ***Gertrude Bell describes mapping the borders of the new country.***

STUDYING PEOPLE

+ Ahead of her time

+ Preserving cultures

Gertrude usually traveled as a tourist, simply for enjoyment. However, she also believed it was important to keep detailed accounts of the people she met in the Middle East. The study of the culture of different peoples in a scientific way is called ethnography. Gertrude's notes were the first of their kind. They gave accurate details about **nomadic** tribes who were unknown in the West.

Did you know ?

Gertrude found learning Arabic difficult. The sounds of Arabic are hard for non-Arabs to reproduce. Gertrude's ability to speak Arabic helped the British during the negotiations to create Iraq.

Hanging at Home

Gertrude's privileged lifestyle meant that she was used to luxury. However, she claimed that she was never happier than when sleeping out in the desert with millions of stars above her.

PITCHING CAMP

- Carries everything with her
- Lives comfortably in the desert

Gertrude traveled in style, accompanied by servants who set up her camp (left). Sometimes she packed a traveling canvas bath along with her collapsible canvas bed. To protect herself from sand flies, she made herself a sleeping bag out of muslin. She also took silver candlesticks and a **dinner service** for eating, so that she could enjoy a proper meal every evening—when there was enough food!

TRAVEL UPDATE

Cover Up!

★ If you're traveling in the Middle East, try covering your head! To protect her head from the desert sun, Gertrude sometimes wore a keffiyeh over her hat. This was a traditional Arab headdress of white cloth. Other times she just wore a big hat (right, in white). Unlike traditional Muslim women, who wore them for religious reasons, Gertrude never wore a veil. Some Muslim women wore veils when they were with Gertrude. This was a mark of respect for Gertrude's political importance.

WHAT'S FOR DINNER?

+ Eat whatever's offered

Although Gertrude took fresh food and supplies into the desert (left), it usually ran out quickly. She soon learned to eat or drink whatever was available. Local tribesmen often slaughtered a sheep to offer to her. Even the eyeballs were eaten. Rice, bread, figs, and soured milk were also local delicacies. Once, Gertrude went for two days without drinking water. Finally, she had no choice but to drink from pools full of worms and insects. To make it easier, she pretended that she was drinking lemonade from the local **bazaars**.

Did you know ?

Gertrude usually took armed soldiers to protect her on her trips into the desert. Some of the remote tribes had a reputation for attacking strangers who entered their territory.

DON'T BE RUDE

★ **Gertrude causes offense**

★ **Learns new manners**

The way of life in the Middle East was very different from the life Gertrude had back home. Once, she accidentally caused offense by leaving a tribe before sharing the meal they had prepared for her. This was considered to be very rude. After that mistake, she learned to rely on her guides to teach her the customs of different peoples. She often carried gifts, such as pistols, as presents for her hosts.

Meeting and Greeting

On Gertrude's many travels in the Middle East, she met many influential local leaders. However, she was equally happy talking to ordinary Arab tribesmen and women around the campfire.

A FIERCE REPUTATION

- **Gertrude meets the Druze**
- **They make her welcome**

The Druze (right) were a tribe from the Levant who were fighting for independence from the Ottoman Empire. The Druze followed their own religion, which was loosely based on Islam. They had a reputation as fierce warriors, but on her first visit to the Middle East, Gertrude became friends with their chief, Yahya Beg. The Druze were surprised to see a female traveler. They called her a "traveling queen." Gertrude was always made welcome in Druze territory.

DESERT NOMADS

- **Bedouin reject authority**
- **Still roam the desert**

The Bedouin (left) are nomadic peoples who still live in the deserts of the Middle East. They speak Arabic, and their lives have changed little since Gertrude first met them more than 100 years ago. The Bedouin rejected all authority. All tribe members were related to each other, and tribal loyalty caused frequent fights with other tribes.

ARAB SELF-RULE

+ Gertrude supports Arabs

+ But also British rule!

Gertrude met many Arab leaders, such as Fahd Beg of the Anazeh tribe of Bedouin (right, front left). She was impressed by such men and believed that the Arabs should have the right to rule themselves. However, she also shared many values with her fellow Britons. She believed that European countries had the right to build empires around the world.

THE FIRST KING OF IRAQ

+ From rebel leader to king

+ Chosen by Gertrude!

With the end of the Ottoman Empire after World War I, the British created the new state of Iraq in 1921. The British needed a ruler to unify the country. Gertrude suggested the rebel leader, Amir Faisal (left). Faisal became the first king. Gertrude hoped he could unite Iraq's Sunni and Shia Muslims. The two groups followed different branches of Islam.

A POWER STRUGGLE

☛ Arab chiefs seek power

☛ Gertrude backs the winner

During the early part of the twentieth century, Ottoman power weakened in the Arabian Peninsula. A power struggle developed between two local Arab chiefs, Ibn Rashid and Ibn Saud. The Ottomans supported Ibn Rashid, with whom Gertrude was friendly. However, she also befriended Ibn Saud, because she thought he would play an important part in Arabia's future. Gertrude was right. Ibn Saud overthrew Ibn Rashid and founded the House of Saud, which still rules Saudi Arabia today.

Running the Empire

Britain took control of parts of the Middle East after World War I. Gertrude's knowledge of the region meant she became involved in advising British officials. She was no longer just a tourist.

RULERS OF THE WORLD

- **Representing the Empire**
- **Setting an example**

When Gertrude traveled, the British Empire covered much of the world. When British **colonial** officials of Gertrude's class went overseas, they lived as if they were still in Great Britain (above). They dressed the same, ate the same food, and played the same sports. It was one of the ways the British tried to show their colonial subjects the supposed superiority of British culture.

VISITING THE VICEROY

★ **Senior British official in India**

India was one of the most important parts of the British Empire. The **Viceroy** of India, Charles Hardinge, was a friend of Gertrude's. India included the largest population of Muslims in the world. During World War I, Hardinge feared that an Arab revolt against the Ottomans would cause tension between the Muslim Middle East and Hindu India. Gertrude traveled to India in 1916 to reassure him that any new Arab state would not be hostile toward India.

T.E. LAWRENCE

+ Known as "Lawrence of Arabia"

Gertrude met Thomas Edward Lawrence (right, 1888–1935) on an archaeological dig in 1911. They became friends because of their shared love of the Middle East. Lawrence became known as "Lawrence of Arabia" because of his adventures in World War I. He joined the Arab revolt led by Ibn Saud against the Ottomans. Gertrude also supported the Arabs. When the British did not give the Arabs independence after the war, Gertrude and Lawrence were both upset. However, Gertrude believed that the creation of Iraq would help to create self-rule for some Arabs.

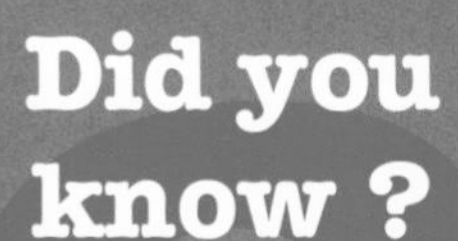

Did you know ?

After World War I, Great Britain and powers such as France and the United States took a close interest in the Middle East. That was partly because the region held large reserves of oil. Oil was in great demand, as it was needed to fuel gasoline engines.

FUTURE PRIME MINISTER

- **Churchill is Secretary of State for War**
- **Calls Cairo Conference in 1921**

Sir Winston Churchill (left, 1874–1965) played a key role in British politics for 50 years and led Great Britain in World War II. During the founding of Iraq, Churchill gathered British officials in Cairo, Egypt, to decide British policy in the Middle East. Because Gertrude was now an advisor to Sir Percy Cox, Churchill asked her to attend. She was the only woman among the 40 delegates.

I Love Nature

Gertrude loved being outdoors. As a child she roamed around her home in northeast England. As an adult she roamed the deserts of the Middle East.

Climbing

Gertrude was the first mountaineer to climb the peaks of the Engelhörner range, which was considered impossible. One of the mountains was named "Gertrude's Peak" after her!

COUNTRY PURSUITS

- Brought up outdoors
- Hunting and fishing

Gertrude's childhood was spent outdoors. She rode ponies from an early age and was known as a brave and fearless rider. She often rode horses in hunts (right). On family holidays to Scotland she learned to fish and climb rocks. The family home was big enough for long games of hide and seek. Whenever Gertrude went back to England, she went back to her family home.

GREEN FINGERS

- ★ Grows flowers as a child
- ★ New flowers in the desert

Gertrude prided herself on her knowledge of and skill at growing flowers. The Middle East had different flowers from Great Britain. Gertrude loved the exotic flowers of Tehran and delighted in the flowers that bloomed on the Jordanian plain after the rains (left). She said that she did not recognize up to nine-tenths of the desert flowers.

Weather Forecast

BEAUTIFUL BUT DEADLY!

Gertrude learned to see the desert in the same way local peoples saw it—as beautiful but dangerous. She loved looking at the stars and sleeping outdoors. But she also realized how dangerous the desert could be. The sun was blazing hot during the daytime, but at night the temperature could fall to near freezing. Gertrude learned to respect the extreme temperatures of the desert.

"Sheets and sheets of varied and exquisite color – purple, white, yellow, and the brightest blue and fields of scarlet ranunculus." *Gertrude describes the flowers of the desert.*

My Explorer Journal

★ Using information in this book, write a holiday advertisement to get people to visit the desert. What might you say to persuade them to visit an environment that can be hostile?

MARSH ARABS

★ **Lifestyle based on reeds**

★ **Reed homes, reed houses**

The Marsh Arabs lived in the swamps along the many rivers of what is now southern Iraq. When Gertrude visited them, she learned how the Marsh Arabs used the tall, woody reeds from the river to make their homes. The houses floated on beds of reeds. The Marsh Arabs also used reeds to make boats (left) and virtually everything else they needed.

Did you know ?

In the late 1900s, the Iraqi government persecuted the Marsh Arabs. The marshes where the people lived were drained. The wetlands turned into desert. Today, only around 1,600 people live in the traditional way.

Fortune Hunting

Most of the time, Gertrude did not have to worry about money. However, by her later years, the family money had started to run out.

Did you know ?

The Bell family home at Rounton Grange was originally built for Gertrude's grandfather and grandmother. It was designed by a leading architect named Philip Webb.

A RICH FAMILY

+ Industrial fortune

Growing up, Gertrude and her family lived in big houses with many servants (above). When she started traveling, Gertrude was able to buy the best equipment and pay for servants wherever she went. She enjoyed good food and fashionable clothes. However, she often claimed that she was just as happy camping in her tent as sleeping in a luxury hotel.

BESTSELLING AUTHOR

★ Doesn't write for money

★ Wants to keep a record

Gertrude decided to write her first book, *Persian Pictures*, as a way of preserving her memories of her time in Persia. She later enjoyed writing her popular travel book, *The Desert and the Sown* (1907). Gertrude included details of the people she met and the conversations she enjoyed around the campfire. It became a bestseller and made Gertrude famous. Everyone wanted to meet the woman behind the adventures.

CULTURAL TREASURE

- Priceless antiquities
- Revealing the past

Gertrude visited many sites of the ancient world, such as Petra in Jordan (left). For her, old ruins and pieces of old clay were like a form of treasure. Gertrude collected records of the early peoples of Mesopotamia, such as tablets written with some of the world's first writing. Gertrude worked on many digs across the region. She spent the last years of her life collecting more than 3,000 objects for a new museum in Baghdad. The museum opened in June 1926, a month before her death.

LIVING IN LUXURY

+ Sets up the court

After Gertrude helped select Faisal as the first king of Iraq (right), the British government asked her to set up his court. As he settled into his new role, the king expected Gertrude to organize everything for him. That meant she got to live in luxury like the king. However, she found the new king very demanding. In the end, the effort of making sure that he was happy made her sick.

TRAVEL UPDATE

Exchanging Gifts

★ If you're planning to meet lots of people on your travels, try taking some gifts. Many people like robes, rolls of silk, or sweets. Gertrude always made sure she had gifts to give people who offered her hospitality. She also learned to accept any gifts she was offered graciously.

This Isn't What It Said in the Brochure!

Gertrude was a fearless explorer, but even she faced sticky moments. Sometimes a situation demanded her courage. At other times, it took all her diplomacy and experience to deal with a possible problem.

ROBBED!

- Intruder in tent
- Steals priceless belongings

In the middle of the night on May 28, 1909, Gertrude was woken up by a noise in one of the other tents. A thief had gotten into the camp. By the time Gertrude raised the alarm, he had escaped. He took her notebooks and photographs, a camera, her clothes, boots, and saddlebags, and some money. Gertrude spoke to her friends among the local people. They found the thief and got everything back except the money—which Gertrude said she did not really care about anyway.

PRISONER!

★ Held by Ibn Rashid

★ Released after almost two weeks

In early 1914, Gertrude was traveling to the fortress city of Hayyil when she was stopped by Ibn Rashid's men. Fearing that Gertrude was helping Ibn Saud to overthrow Rashid, they took Gertrude prisoner for almost two weeks. They held Gertrude prisoner in Ibn Rashid's palace. Just when she thought she would never leave, she was freed and given a bag of gold. She never found out why she was released.

Weather Forecast

WILD WEATHER!

Over the years, Gertrude learned to expect extreme weather in the desert. But on one trip in 1913 the winter weather was much worse than usual. Howling winds, ice, sleet, and fog caused her servants' tent to freeze. They had to light fires to thaw out the canvas. Flash floods sent her camels slipping and falling. In the summer, the heat rose to over 140° Fahrenheit (60°C)—but it was bitterly cold at night.

Did you know ?

Flash floods in the desert often occur after heavy rainfall. The ground is too hard for the water to soak up, so the water runs across the surface of the desert in fast-flowing streams.

DEFYING DEATH

- Suffers serious accidents
- But doesn't stop climbing!

Gertrude's sense of adventure was matched by the excitement of climbing difficult mountains. Nothing intimidated her. Gertrude wore her underclothes or men's pants to climb. She then changed back into her skirt at the base of a mountain. Despite a number of serious accidents, she did not give up climbing. After one accident, Gertrude was left hanging on a rope for 48 hours. Another time, she almost froze to death while descending a mountain after a climb.

End of the Road

Gertrude Bell's last years were spent in the new country of Iraq. She worked to help the new king and to establish the country's first archaeological museum.

A FAMOUS LADY

- Known as "El Khatun"
- At home in Baghdad

By the time of the founding of Iraq in 1921, Arabic people called Gertrude Bell "El Khatun" ("The Lady"). The title was a mark of respect for her role in creating the country. King Faisal called her the greatest woman of all time. She lived in her home in Baghdad (right). However, the way the British created the country also caused problems for the future. It set the territory up without thinking about the different religious and ethnic groups who did not get along. It also created borders that divided deserts that had been open to nomadic peoples for many centuries.

A LASTING LEGACY

- ★ Collects artifacts
- ★ Founds a museum

Gertrude's travels through the Middle East had opened her eyes to its remarkable ancient culture. Fearing that objects that were thousands of years old might be lost forever if they were not saved, Gertrude set about collecting as many as she could for a new museum in Baghdad. Her hard work paid off—the museum opened its first room in June 1926.

SUDDEN DEATH

☛ Dies in her sleep

☛ Aged just 57

Gertrude died suddenly on July 12, 1926, just two days before her 58th birthday. Her death was a tremendous shock. Before she died, Gertrude had faced a number of difficulties. Her beloved brother Hugo had died in February 1926. The Bell family's fortune was running out. More importantly, Gertrude's health was increasingly fragile, and she was losing her energy.

FOUNDING A COUNTRY

+ Gertrude creates Iraq

Gertrude's greatest **legacy** was the creation of Iraq. She helped decide its borders. She knew more about the different tribes living there than any other Westerner of that time. She chose Iraq's first king and the design of its flag. She is the only woman to have played such an important role in the founding of a country. The effects of the creation of Iraq are still being felt today.

A SAD LOSS

★ Large funeral

★ Letter from the King

Gertrude was buried in Baghdad. Her funeral was attended by important government officials and King Faisal. In England, King George V (right) wrote a letter of sympathy to her parents. A special plaque dedicated to her memory was erected in the museum she had founded in Baghdad.

"She was, I think, the greatest woman of our time, and perhaps amongst the greatest of all time." *Scholar and writer Janet Hogarth on her friend, Gertrude Bell.*

GLOSSARY

archaeologist A person who learns about the past by studying old ruins and objects

artifacts Things that have been made by humans, particularly by hand

bazaars Markets in Middle Eastern countries

berth A fixed bunk or sleeping place on a ship

colonial Related to colonies, or regions a country governs outside its own borders

consul An official appointed by a country to live in a foreign country in order to take care of the interests of its citizens there

delegates People chosen to represent other people at a conference

dinner service A set of matching china plates, dishes, bowls, and cups

diplomacy The skill of dealing with people in a sensitive way

diplomat An official who represents a country overseas

dynasty A series of rulers who all come from the same family

edited Prepared material for publication by selecting, sorting, and annotating it

empire A large area ruled by the same ruler

excavation The methodical uncovering of something that is buried

Islamic Related to Islam, the faith of Muslims

legacy Something that is handed down from the past

linguist Someone who is skilled at learning foreign languages

nomadic Describes people who move around with the seasons rather than living in one place

peninsula A long, thin piece of land projecting into a body of water

protectorate A state that is controlled and protected by another. After World War I, parts of the Ottoman Empire in the Middle East became protectorates of Great Britain and France

reserves Underground supplies of oil and natural gas

sidesaddle Sitting on a horse with both legs on the same side of the saddle

viceroy Someone who rules an area on behalf of a monarch

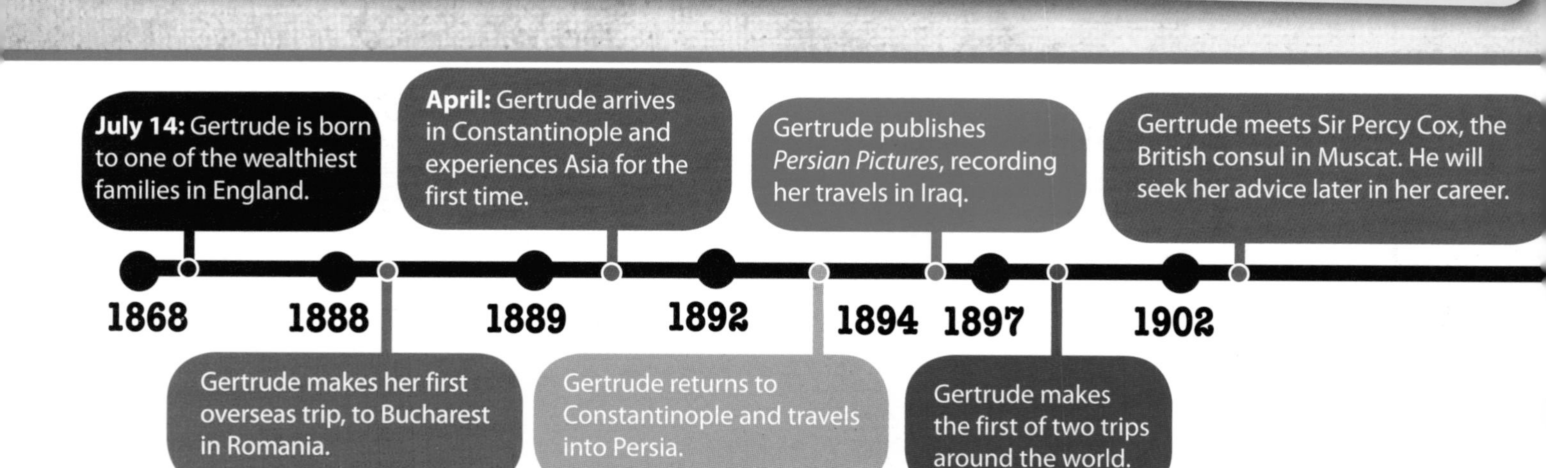

ON THE WEB

biography.yourdictionary.com/gertrude-bell
A biography page about Gertrude Bell for younger readers.

www.theguardian.com/world/2003/mar/12/iraq.jamesbuchan
An article from the British newspaper *The Guardian* about Gertrude's life and her lasting influence on the Middle East.

research.ncl.ac.uk/gertrudecomics/
From Newcastle University, a selection of interesting episodes from Gertrude's life told in comic strips.

literary-destinations.com/authors/gertrude-bell/timeline
A timeline of Gertrude Bell's life and career.

www.theposthole.org/read/article/64
An archaeology journal for students explores Gertrude Bell's archaeology in the Middle East.

BOOKS

Bell, Gertrude. *A Woman in Arabia: The Writings of the Queen of the Desert*. Penguin Classics, 2015.

Howell, Georgina. *Gertrude Bell: Queen of the Desert, Shaper of Nations*. Sarah Crichton Books, 2008.

Roxburgh, Ellis. *The British Empire*. Great Empires. Hachette Kids, 2017.

Sonneborn, Liz. *Iraq*. Enchantment of the World. Children's Press, 2012.

1907

Gertrude writes her best-selling book about Persia, *The Desert and the Sown*.

1909

May 28: While she is camping in the desert, Gertrude's belongings are stolen from a tent during the night.

1911

Gertrude meets T.E. Lawrence on an archaeological dig.

1914

Gertrude is briefly taken prisoner by Ibn Rashid in Arabia.

1919

After World War I, France and Great Britain establish protectorates in the Middle East.

1921

Gertrude attends the Cairo Conference to help set up the new country of Iraq.

1926

June: The first room of the National Museum opens in Baghdad.

July 12: Gertrude dies suddenly of unknown causes at the age of just 57.

INDEX